T0053871

The Little Encyclopedia of

MYTHICAL
HORSES

The Little Encyclopedia of
MYTHICAL HORSES

An **A-to-Z Guide** to

Legendary Steeds

Eliza Berkowitz

Illustrated by Kate Forrester

RUNNING PRESS
PHILADELPHIA

Running Press
Hachette Book Group
1290 Avenue of the Americas, New York, NY 10104
www.runningpress.com
@Running_Press

First Edition: February 2024

Published by Running Press, an imprint of Hachette Book Group, Inc.
The Running Press name and logo are trademarks of Hachette Book Group, Inc.

The Hachette Speakers Bureau provides a wide range of authors for speaking events. To find out more, go to www.hachettespeakersbureau.com or email HachetteSpeakers@hbgusa.com.

Running Press books may be purchased in bulk for business, educational, or promotional use. For more information, please contact your local bookseller or the Hachette Book Group Special Markets Department at Special.Markets@hbgusa.com.

The publisher is not responsible for websites (or their content) that are not owned by the publisher.

Print book cover and interior design by Katie Benezra.
Written by Eliza Berkowitz.

Library of Congress Cataloging-in-Publication Data

Names: Berkowitz, Eliza, author. | Forrester, Kate (Illustrator), illustrator.
Title: The little encyclopedia of mythical horses : an A-to-Z guide to legendary steeds / Eliza Berkowitz ; illustrated by Kate Forrester.
Description: First edition. | Philadelphia : Running Press, an imprint of Perseus Books, LLC, [2024] | Includes bibliographical references and index.
Identifiers: LCCN 2023021575 (print) | LCCN 2023021576 (ebook) | ISBN 9780762484898 (hardcover) | ISBN 9780762486991 (ebook)
Subjects: LCSH: Horses—Mythology—Encyclopedias. | Horses—Folklore—Encyclopedias.
Classification: LCC GR715 .B47 2024 (print) | LCC GR715 (ebook) |
    DDC 398.24/529665503—dc23/eng/20230712
LC record available at https://lccn.loc.gov/2023021575
LC ebook record available at https://lccn.loc.gov/2023021576

ISBNs: 978-0-7624-8489-8 (hardcover), 978-0-7624-8699-1 (ebook)

Printed in the United States of America

LSC-C

Printing 1, 2023

CONTENTS

INTRODUCTION

For thousands of years, horses have played a central role in the stories and folklore of nearly every culture. Horses represented different things to different people—power and status to the ancient Greeks; fertility and prosperity to the Norse; and speed and freedom to the ancient Chinese. In some traditions, horses are also seen as symbols of warriors and military might. In addition, horses are often associated with the divine and the spiritual world, and they are sometimes regarded as messengers or agents of the gods. Even in the present day, horses bring to mind the notion of independence, grace, speed, and energy. We associate them with the natural world and with the wild, untamed spirit of the outdoors.

In the earliest human civilizations, horses were instrumental in the advancement of key areas, such as transportation, warfare, and agriculture. Before travel on horse-pulled chariots, carts, and wagons, humans could only journey as fast as they could walk. Along with the ability to traverse areas more quickly, horse transportation gave warriors a great advantage—it was now easier to carry supplies and artillery, plus surprising the enemy with a sneak attack was possible. In terms of agriculture, horses made the job of plowing and cultivating the land much quicker, and they did so with little adverse effect on the environment.

Some people have a strong emotional connection to horses. They may find comfort and solace in spending time in the presence of such beauty and grace. Others are drawn to their power and mystique. In therapeutic settings, horses have the ability to help people suffering from a huge range of physical and emotional illnesses.

The influence of the horse on literature, art, and popular culture cannot be overstated. Horses have been featured in a wide range of films, television shows, and other forms of media, and they often play important roles in the stories that are told. In media for younger audiences, horses are often featured as the main characters. Shows like *My Little Pony* and *Spirit Riding Free* capture kids' attention with stories of adventure and friendship. There are a plethora of science fiction and fantasy stories for horse lovers young and old. Horses are often featured in historical dramas and other types of films set in the past, where they are used to help tell stories about days gone by.

Horses also play a key role in many different sports. Millions of people enjoy watching and betting on horse racing, which is a multibillion-dollar industry. Polo, played on horseback, is another popular sport, especially among the wealthy and elite. It is often associated with high society and luxury. Equestrian events can take many different forms, including dressage, which involves performing a series of precise movements and maneuvers with a horse; and show jumping, in which an athlete jumps over a series of obstacles on horseback. In fact, equestrian events are even included in the Olympic Games and have been since 1912.

With their long-standing popularity and sustained presence in the world, horses aren't going anywhere. That is due, in part, to the adoration of unicorns and other mythical horses. Unicorns are a mainstay in every conceivable product for children—from clothes to books to toys to accessories and more. Unicorns are everywhere. Children may be drawn to the unicorn's magical abilities, graceful physicality, and calm nature, but unicorns and other mythical horses aren't just for kids. Their magical energy and sparkly vibes will continue to captivate our imagination for the foreseeable future.

Although the unicorn is perhaps the first thing that comes to mind when one thinks "mythical horse," there are actually so many to be discovered from folktales all around the world. Some are more well-known than others, but each offers a fascinating peek into the stories and beliefs that influenced a culture's history and its people.

MYTHICAL
HORSES

A

AGRICULTURAL POWERHOUSE

THROUGHOUT HISTORY, REAL horses have played an essential role in the development of agriculture. Capable of completing farm labor much more efficiently than humans, horses were used to herd other animals, carry harvested goods and other materials, and plow fields. And since they worked so much quicker than people, horses allowed farmers to increase productivity. They could expand the number of crops grown and produce more of each.

The invention of the tractor in the late 1800s changed how farms operated. This powerful machinery was capable of cultivating land faster than horses could. Farmers no longer needed to dedicate so much land to the oats they had been growing to feed the horses, so space was freed up to plant new crops. There were many advantages to adopting this new technology.

Horse labor on farms did not disappear completely, however. There were still some benefits to keeping working horses as well as drawbacks to using heavy equipment. Horses had much less of an impact on the land, whereas heavy machinery could damage the soil by compacting it. And tractors required fuel, which needed to be purchased, affecting a farm's bottom line.

Today, most farms use machinery to cultivate the land, but some farms, especially smaller farms, still utilize horses. You are most likely to see horses working on agritourism farms, helping to bring in tourists for hayrides, horseback riding lessons, or trail rides.

AMERIGO

ON THE EVENING of December 5, children throughout the Netherlands and Belgium observe a curious tradition. Before bed, they sing songs and leave a shoe that contains a carrot and some hay by their chimney. These items are left as gifts for Amerigo, the flying white horse of Sinterklaas. A familiar figure in the Low Countries, Sinterklaas is modeled after Saint Nicholas, a character from European folklore who was also the basis for the figure we know presently as Santa Claus. The two holiday patriarchs have a lot in common: they both wear red and white; they both have white hair and long beards; and they both keep track of who has been good or bad every year. One notable difference, however, is that Santa has eight flying reindeer to help him get around and Amerigo shoulders the burden alone, carrying Sinterklaas from house to house to deliver all his gifts.

In the Netherlands, a televised event in mid-November kicks off the holiday season. Actors playing the characters Sinterklaas, Amerigo, and Sinterklaas's helper, Zwarte Piet, arrive on a steamboat from Spain, then Amerigo carries Sinterklaas in appearances throughout Amsterdam to build excitement for the upcoming holiday. The same horse played Amerigo for many years, until it passed away. In 2019, a new horse character was introduced, named Ozosnel, who replaced Amerigo, taking the reins to continue the beloved annual tradition.

ANATOMY OF A HORSE

HORSES HAVE A complex anatomy that supports their capacity for power and speed. They have evolved over millions of years to be able to run superfast and traverse long distances. Here are some of the horse's unique features:

- The horse has a large head with sensitive ears and a strong jaw to help with chewing grass. Its sizable eyes are set on the sides of its head, which provides the horse with a wide field of vision.

- A horse's neck is long and flexible, connected to the body like a lever. Well-developed muscles in the neck help it maneuver and balance the considerable weight of the head and neck on the body.

- The body of the horse is compact with a broad chest. A flexible spine helps a horse move smoothly when running.

- The horse's legs are long and well-muscled, with large shock-absorbing hooves. The hind legs are particularly powerful, which is why you should never stand behind a horse.

- The long tail of a horse helps with balance. It is also used to swat away flies and other insects.

- The mane of a horse is made of long hair. Depending on a horse's breed, its mane can have different textures and colors.

- A horse's teeth are uniquely adapted for grinding down the plants they eat.

ARION

NOT TO BE confused with the poet and musician Arion (a real-life historical figure from ancient Greece who, according to legend, was saved from death by a music-loving dolphin), the equine Arion was an immortal talking horse known for his speed and considerable size. He was the child of Poseidon, king of the sea, earthquakes, and horses, and Demeter, goddess of the harvest. Poseidon had taken a liking to Demeter, who at the time was preoccupied with the search for her missing daughter, Persephone. Unwilling to be deterred, Poseidon aggressively pursued Demeter, who changed form into a mare in an attempt to hide from him among a group of grazing horses. When she was discovered by Poseidon, he turned himself into a stallion and forced himself on her, an event that led to the birth of Arion and his sister, the nymph Despoena.

Arion played an important role during the expedition of the Seven Against Thebes, a fight between the seven champions and the powerful city of Thebes. Oedipus had been the city's king, and after his death there was a struggle between his twin sons for power. The sons came up with a plan to take turns ruling Thebes, but Eteocles refused to cede the throne when it was Polyneices's turn to rule. As a result, a group was mobilized to reclaim the throne, but only one warrior was able to survive. Adrastus had the good fortune and presence of mind to be able to call on his swift horse, Arion, who carried him to safety.

ÁRVAKR AND ALSVIÐR

ALTHOUGH NOT THE most famous horses to appear in Norse mythology (that honor goes to **Sleipnir**, covered on page 94, the eight-legged horse ridden by the god Odin), Árvakr and

Alsviðr did the important work of pulling the
chariot belonging to Sól, the sun, across the sky
each day. (Sól's brother, Máni, the moon, also
rode in a horse-drawn chariot, though his horses
were not named.)

Árvakr translates to "early riser," and
Alsviðr means "swift." The horses had to be
swift to outrun the wolves that chased Sól and
Máni each day and night. Many believed that
the wolves would hunt the sun and moon until
they eventually consumed them, at which point
the world would be plunged into darkness and
a series of disasters would lead to the world's
destruction. This event, called Ragnarök, was
a prophecy of how the world ends. To make
Árvakr and Alsviðr's hard work a little more
comfortable, the gods gave each horse wind bags
under their shoulders to provide a cool breeze
for each horse to enjoy.

The horse siblings appeared in the *Prose
Edda*, the Icelandic body of text that serves as the

primary source for our present-day understanding of Germanic mythology. Images of Sól, pulled by Árvakr and Alsviðr, have been discovered in artifacts dating back to the Bronze Age.

B

BAI MA

HORSES PLAYED A significant role in traditional Chinese culture. They were used for transportation and also to aid in military endeavors. Considered a symbol of wealth and power, they were often given as gifts to important officials and other high-ranking individuals. Valued for their beauty and grace, horses were often portrayed in Chinese art and literature, and were an important part of Chinese mythology for their

association with the gods and goddesses of the sky, the earth, and the underworld.

According to legend, a white horse named Bai Ma was instrumental in bringing Buddhism to China. In 64 CE, Emperor Mingdi of the Eastern Han dynasty sent a group of men to study Buddhism in western regions, with the goal of bringing back the knowledge they obtained. After three years, the men returned to China with two Indian monks, She Moteng and Zhu Falan. They also had with them Buddhist

Based on the fabled character Bai Ma from Chinese mythology, **Bai Long Ma** appears in the sixteenth century novel *Journey to the West*. Written by Wu Cheng'en, this adventure story expands on the legend that describes how Buddhism was introduced to China. In the book, Buddhist monk Xuanzang sets out on a pilgrimage from China to India to find religious texts. On his fourteen-year journey, he is protected by three disciples and a white dragon horse named Bai Long Ma. This winged creature had the body of a horse and the head of a dragon and was covered in scales.

scriptures and statues that had been carried by Bai Ma. The horse's help was instrumental— without Bai Ma, it would have been impossible to carry these invaluable items back to China.

To recognize Bai Ma's contributions, the emperor ordered a temple be built in the horse's honor. Named the White Horse Temple, it is the oldest Buddhist temple in China. In front of the temple, they erected a large statue of Bai Ma. Visitors travel to Bai Ma Si in the Luolong District to visit the temple, learn about Buddhism, and view the original scriptures that were transported almost two thousand years ago.

BAKU

ORIGINATING IN JAPANESE folklore, the baku is a supernatural creature that helps humans by consuming their nightmares. Descriptions of the baku vary, but oftentimes they include parts of different animals, like the horse, elephant, lion, cow, and tiger, merged into a single being. Its followers believed that the baku was capable of turning a person's devoured bad dreams into good fortune and peace. A picture of a baku in a bedroom was said to ward off evil spirits and prevent a person from having fitful sleep. And it was not unusual for a child to have a baku stuffed toy for the same purpose.

While generally seen as benevolent and helpful, sometimes bakus were thought to disrupt a person's sleep, or consume all of a person's dreams, good or bad, depriving that person of the potential positive effects of dreaming.

It was common for the baku to be represented in traditional Japanese art, especially in a style of woodblock prints called ukiyo-e. The baku also makes frequent appearances in various forms of modern popular culture. In the world of Pokémon, there is a baku character named Drowzee, and bakus show up often in Japanese manga and anime.

BALIUS AND XANTHUS

APPEARING IN GREEK mythology, Balius and Xanthus were immortal horses born to Zephyrus, god of the west wind and messenger of spring, and the harpy Podarge. (Harpies were half-woman, half-bird creatures sent by the gods to punish anyone who angered them.) The horses were described as swift, with beautiful, long manes. Their names describe their coloring—*balius* is a word that, when used to describe horses, means "dappled," and *xanthus* means "reddish-yellow."

Poseidon gave these horses to King Peleus as a wedding gift when he married the sea goddess Thetis. Later, Peleus would give Balius and Xanthus to his son, Achilles, who relied on them in battle.

During the Trojan War, Achilles lent his horses to his close friend (and possibly lover), Patroclus, to pull his chariot in battle. Achilles also gave Patroclus his armor to wear, a mistake that he would later regret. The two men had spent much of their lives together and were inseparable, so when Patroclus was struck by an arrow and killed, Achilles was distraught. The Trojan prince Hector had been aiming for Achilles but mistook Patroclus for him, because of his armor. In his grief, Achilles blamed Balius and Xanthus for his friend's death. The goddess Hera, Zeus's wife, stepped in and gave Xanthus the ability to speak so he could explain

how Patroclus was killed. Xanthus insisted that he and his brother had nothing to do with his death, and then prophesized that Achilles would die at the hands of a god and a man. The horse's prediction turned out to be true—the arrow that later ended Achilles's life was shot by Paris, a Trojan prince guided by the god Apollo.

Balius and Xanthus were devastated by Achilles's death at the end of the Trojan War. In their grief, they refused to eat. They were eventually taken to the Elysian Fields, the resting place of heroic and virtuous souls, and granted immortality. There, they enjoyed their lives in peace and happiness.

BAYARD

THE LEGEND OF Bayard evolved from medieval French epic poems. These poems told the tales of Charlemagne, ruler over much of Western Europe during the Middle Ages, whose magical horse had exceptional strength and the ability to understand human speech, and could grow his body to accommodate extra passengers, even if that meant an entire army. Bayard belonged to the legendary knight Renaud de Montauban. Together, the two went on many great adventures, and Bayard became a trusted counsel to his owner. Bayard continued to appear in legends as they were told and retold, eventually becoming a notable figure in French and Belgian folklore.

Bayard (called Ros Beiaard in Belgium) was named for his "bay" coat of reddish-brown color. He was said to have the ability to change color and blend in with his surroundings, rendering him almost impossible to see. In early texts, he was described as having a slender build, broad shoulders, a muscular chest, and a silver star on his forehead.

Statues of Bayard can be found in the Netherlands, France, Belgium, and Denmark. He is usually depicted with four men on his back, as in the medieval tale *The Four Sons of Aymon*. The most recent Bayard statue, a large sculpture made from strips of metal, was erected in Bogny-sur-Meuse, France, in 2018.

CELERIS

THE WINGED HORSE Pegasus is an enduring figure in Greek mythology, but his brother Celeris is less widely known. Some sources say that

Celeris was the son of Pegasus, but they are more commonly referred to as siblings. Celeris is a foal with a talent for taming horses. He was given as a gift to Castor, a skilled horseman, by the god Mercury.

In proportion to his minimal presence in the classical myths, Celeris is represented by the constellation Equuleus, one of the smallest, dullest constellations in the night sky. Overshadowed by the much larger, brighter constellation Pegasus, the best way to spot these neighboring constellations is to find Enif, the bright star that sits at Pegasus's nose. From there, look slightly southwest and you will find Equuleus. The constellation forms the shape of a horse's head.

CENTAURS

THE PRESENCE OF centaurs in mythology can be traced back to ancient Sumer. In the earliest depictions, centaurs had wings and scorpion tails, and they were the protectors of Kur, the underworld. As time went on, centaurs evolved into the race of half-man, half-horse creatures that we think of today, who lived in tribes on Mount Pelion. These centaurs were known to be unpredictable and violent, especially toward women. Bound by their primal instincts, they ate raw meat, drank strong wine, and generally acted belligerently. It was not uncommon for centaurs to stampede through the countryside, uprooting trees and destroying vegetation. Centaurs represented the uncivilized side of humankind.

Depicted as the head and upper torso of a man with the body and legs of a horse, centaurs in Greek mythology are perhaps best remembered for their battle with a neighboring

mountain tribe called the Lapiths. Ixion, king of the Lapiths, invited the centaurs to his son's wedding. The centaur guests were well-behaved at first but became unruly as the party wore on. They insulted the other guests, harassed the bridesmaids, and tried to make off with the bride. The Lapith men, angered by this blatant show of disrespect, attacked the centaurs, who, in their drunken state, were not prepared to fight back. Many centaurs were wounded or killed, and those that remained were driven from Greece by the Lapiths. This battle has been depicted in countless pieces of art, most notably in the Michelangelo sculpture *Battle of the Centaurs*. The fight is said to represent the human struggle between civilized behavior and barbaric instincts.

In modern times, centaurs make frequent appearances in literature, especially in the science fiction and fantasy genres. Centaurs appear in some of the most popular media franchises,

Centaurides are female centaurs, and although they are infrequently mentioned in ancient literature, they do show up in Greek and Roman art. These half-female, half-horse creatures were renowned for their beauty and, like their male counterparts, were known to be rowdy and wild.

One notable centauride was the centaur Cyllarus's lover, named Hylonome. Their love story ended tragically when, during the battle with the Lapiths, Cyllarus was struck with a spear. He collapsed and Hylonome threw herself on the spear to die alongside her love.

including the Harry Potter books and movies, the Star Wars movies, and the book series Percy Jackson and the Olympians.

CHIRON

CHIRON, THE CENTAUR king, was known for
having a drastically different temperament and
reputation from that of other centaurs, who
were known to be rowdy and coarse. In contrast,
Chiron was wise, kind, and knowledgeable.
His patient nature and knowledge of various
subjects made him an excellent teacher. He
tutored and guided many of the heroes of Greek
mythology as young men, including Heracles,
Jason, and Achilles.

Chiron was also a healer with a vast knowledge about medicine. Although he had lots of
experience helping others when they fell ill, he
was unable to heal himself after he was acciden-
tally pricked with one of Heracles's poisoned
arrows. The arrow's tip had been dipped in
Hydra's blood, making it a deadly weapon that
caused excruciating pain. Chiron was immortal, which left him facing an eternity of pain

and anguish from his wound. He begged the gods to allow him to perish, rather than face a life of unending misery. Zeus, Heracles's father, granted Chiron's request and allowed him to die. In tribute, he was placed in the sky as the constellation Centaurus.

Chiron's legacy is enduring. In astrology, the asteroid Chiron is associated with past traumas or vulnerabilities. Depending where the asteroid falls on your birth chart, a person can better understand and heal emotional wounds. Chiron has also influenced modern literature. Published in 1962, John Updike's *The Centaur* is a National Book Award–winning retelling of the story of Chiron, featuring the backdrop of a Pennsylvania high school to represent Mount Olympus.

CHUMUR DEKI

ALSO KNOWN AS the Iron-Legged Steed, the sound of Chumur Deki's hooves was considered a bad omen in Chitrali mythology. (The Chitrali people lived in a region called Chitral, which is in modern-day Pakistan.) According to legend, despair would befall anyone unlucky enough to lay eyes on Chumur Deki. This evil steed was but one of many mythical creatures that the Chitrali believed in. Some, like the fairies who aided warriors or the pixies who ushered in autumn, were thought of as benevolent. Others, like Khapisi, the night hag, or Nihang, an aquatic dragon, were regarded with fear, as was the case with the demonic horse Chumur Deki.

COLTPIXIE

IN ENGLISH FOLKLORE, a coltpixie is a sly goblin that takes the form of a horse. They neigh to other horses to trick them into veering off course. They also are known to attack boys who steal apples from orchards.

CYPRIAN CENTAURS

NATIVE TO THE island of Cyprus, Cyprian Centaurs were different from other centaurs in Greek mythology in that they had bull horns atop their heads. Otherwise, they looked much the same, with the head and torso of a human and the hindquarters of a horse.

Cyprian Centaurs came about as the result of Zeus's failed attempt to sleep with Aphrodite, the goddess of love and sexuality, thought to be the most beautiful goddess of all. Aphrodite (who in some stories is Zeus's daughter) was able to evade Zeus's advances, but not before he spilled some of his semen on the ground. The goddess Gaia, personified as the Earth, became pregnant, and the Cyprian Centaurs were the resulting offspring.

D

DUB SAINGLEND

IN IRISH FOLKLORE, Cú Chulainn is a brave and powerful war hero, famous for his incredible strength and skill in battle. His chariot was pulled by two horses, **Grey of Macha** (see page 37) and the lesser-known and lesser-appreciated Dub Sainglend. By all accounts, Dub Sainglend was Cú Chulainn's least favorite of his two steeds. In the story of Cú Chulainn's death, Dub Sainglend ran in fear, never to be seen again, while Grey of Macha, Cú Chulainn's braver and more beloved companion, stayed and was struck.

DYAUS PITA

A RECURRING CONCEPT in mythology is that of the "sky god," otherwise known as a single male deity with the power to rule a kingdom. In Greek mythology, there is the powerful and majestic Zeus. His counterpart in Roman mythology is Jupiter. In ancient Hindu mythology, Dyaus Pita is the supreme being and the father of all Hindu gods. Like Zeus, he is a lightning-bolt-wielding provider and protector.

The Rigveda is one of the four sacred ancient texts (called Vedas) that detail early Hinduism. In it, Dyaus Pita is sometimes depicted as a night sky in the form of a black horse wearing a pearl necklace. Other times, he presents as a bull. The ideas expressed in the Vedas have been outdated for centuries; present-day Hinduism contains very few of the religion's early beliefs.

E

EMBARR

NIAMH, GODDESS OF beauty and brightness in Irish mythology, had a special horse, Embarr (sometimes called Enbarr), who could walk on land and water. Together, the fair maiden and her trusty horse embarked on a quest to find a husband for Niamh. They traveled a great distance, eventually arriving in County Kerry, where they approached a group of men. Setting her sights on Oisín, a celebrated war hero and poet, Niamh explained that she was looking for a husband. Charmed by her beauty and gentle nature, Oisín was all too happy to oblige, and with his father's reluctant blessing, they set off together for the Land of the Young. Riding on Embarr, they traveled straight into the sea, riding atop the water past many strange lands.

In the Land of the Young, Niamh and Oisín shared a beautiful life. The couple married, had a daughter, and lived happily in the eternal springlike climate. But after three years, Oisín started to feel homesick and asked to go back to County Kerry to see family and familiar places. Niamh explained that he could never again set foot on mortal soil, but said that if he could remain on Embarr's back, the horse could take him to his homeland.

Time passed differently in the Land of the Young. In the three years Oisín spent there, three hundred years had passed in the mortal world. Everything and everyone he knew were long gone. He stopped to help a group of men who were struggling with a boulder, and as he leaned over, the strap holding him to the horse broke and Oisín tumbled to the ground. In an instant, time caught up with him and Oisín aged hundreds of years. Embarr ran off, frightened by the commotion, and in a short time Oisín died, never having the chance to see his beloved Niamh again.

EQUESTRIAN SPORTS

MANY ATHLETES WHO are passionate about horses participate in equestrian sports. National and international competitions, including the Olympics, give riders a chance to compete against other best-in-class equestrians. In the world of equestrian sports, there are three main disciplines in which riders compete: dressage, show jumping, and hunter trials.

In dressage competitions, riders perform a set of moves that show off the horse's athleticism and their own understanding of the horse's behavior and movements. It is sometimes referred to as "horse ballet" because of the beauty and elegance with which the moves are executed.

Show jumping involves guiding a horse to complete a set of jumps over obstacles on a course. Each rider is timed, and points are taken away for knocking over an obstacle or failing to successfully clear a jump.

For riders who prefer a less formal setting or the freedom to navigate obstacles on natural terrain, hunter trials replicate the conditions that a hunter might encounter, with areas of fallen logs, obtrusive gates, and even ditches or water crossings to clear. Riders and horses are given marks based on their style, pace, and accuracy.

Having an understanding of horse behavior and proper riding techniques, plus the dedication and discipline to maintain a strict practice regimen, are a few of the qualities needed to succeed in equestrian sports.

In the 1928 Winter Olympics in Saint Moritz, Switzerland, a sport called Skijöring was demonstrated for the first (and only) time. This Scandinavian sport involves skiing while being pulled along by reins attached to a horse, pony, or dog.

G

GREY OF MACHA

KNOWN AS THE king of all horses in Irish-Celtic mythology, Grey of Macha (also called Macha's Grey or Liath Macha) was one of two horses to pull the chariot of the great warrior Cú Chulainn. Detailed in the Ulster Cycle, which chronicles the legends of early medieval Ireland, Cú Chulainn had a number of magical advantages that helped him succeed in battle. His spear, called Gáe Bulga, was crafted from sea monster bones and inflicted an extra thirty wounds with each strike. His sword, called Caladbolg, was nimble and unbreakable. His horses, Grey of Macha and a black horse named **Dub Sainglend** (see page 30), were exceptionally fast, loyal, and well trained. They pulled the chariot that carried Cú Chulainn into battle.

In one version of Cú Chulainn's death, he summoned his horse for battle, but for the very first time Macha refused to listen. The horse knew there was trickery taking place, and he cried tears of blood for his inability to protect his master. After the third attempt at getting the horse to obey, Macha relented; he drew the chariot and they rode toward the battle. Three magical spears had been created to kill Cú Chulainn. The first spear hit Láeg, their loyal charioteer. The next spear hit Grey of Macha, which sent his faithful companion Cú Chulainn into a rage. The last spear hit Cú Chulainn in the stomach, but he refused to lie down and die. In an attempt to resist death, he used his intestines, which had fallen out of his wound, to tie himself upright against a rock. The great warrior was so feared that even after his death, no one was brave enough to go near the body. After three days, they sent a raven to perch on Cú Chulainn, and when he did not move, they knew he was dead.

GRINGOLET

SIR GAWAIN, TRUSTED nephew of King Arthur in Arthurian legend, was a much respected and virtuous knight. Featured in many Middle English poems as a loyal and beloved figure with an impeccable moral compass, he enjoyed

the companionship of his magnificent horse, Gringolet, with whom he had many adventures.

There are many conflicting stories about how Gawain came to own his horse. In one story, Gawain won Gringolet from Clarion, a Saxon king. In another, Gringolet is a gift to Gawain from the fairy Esclarmonde.

Gringolet's name means either "handsome and hardy" or "white and hardy." He was such a special horse that he is the only animal companion in Arthurian texts to be given a name. He was also given fanciful clothing—he was described as being adorned in gold and sparkling in the sun. Although he was a sturdy and agile warhorse, he met an untimely end during battle. Gawain was devastated to lose his trusted friend.

H

HAYAGRĪVA

IN BUDDHIST MYTHOLOGY, a horse-faced god named Hayagrīva appears as one of the many incarnations of the deity Vishnu, the god of preservation who restores balance to the world. Depending on the text, Hayagrīva is portrayed as either benevolent and wise or as a demon who steals the four Vedas (Hindu texts) in order to prevent humankind from having them.

THE HEADLESS HORSEMAN

IN WASHINGTON IRVING'S 1820 short story "The Legend of Sleepy Hollow," an unsophisticated schoolteacher named Ichabod Crane

sets out to earn the affection of Katrina Van Tassel, the daughter of a wealthy landowner. Crane is not alone in his desire to win Katrina's love; another suitor, named Brom Bones, is also hoping to get closer to her. In an effort to scare Crane away, Brom Bones appears to Crane as he is heading home from a party at the Van Tassels'. Riding on a black horse, he makes himself look like a headless figure and chases Crane through the woods, throwing at Crane a round pumpkin that he mistakes for the headless man's decapitated head. Terrified, Crane rides out of town and is never heard from again.

The real town of Sleepy Hollow is located in Westchester County, New York, about twenty-five miles north of Manhattan. There, an eighteen-foot-tall metal sculpture of the Headless Horseman and Ichabod Crane is the most-visited attraction in town.

HENGROEN

HENGROEN WAS ONE of King Arthur's stallions.
In a group of medieval texts called the Welsh
Triads, Hengroen was named as the horse that
accompanied King Arthur to the battlefield of
Camlann during what would be the king's last
battle. The only survivor was Saint Cynwyl, a
warrior saint of the Carmarthernshire region.
Hengroen carried the wounded soldier out of
Camlann at the end of the fight.

HIPPALECTRYON

THE HIPPALECTRYON IS an unusual hybrid creature
from Greek mythology. It has the forequarters
of a horse, and the tail, wings, and back legs of
a rooster. Hippalectryon means "cock horse" or
"rooster horse," from the Greek words *hippos* and
alektryôn. Some sources depict the hippalectryon

as a fierce and powerful flying creature while others describe it as more of a silly or mischievous animal. The creature only appears in ancient Athenian art and may be an early representation of the winged horse **Pegasus** (see page 80).

HIPPOCAMPUS

APPEARING IN MYTHOLOGY from different cultures, including Greek, Roman, and Phoenician, the hippocampus is a horse of the sea. Depicted with the head and front legs of a horse and the body of a fish, hippocampi were created by the Greek god Poseidon, ruler of the sea. Known for their strength and speed underwater, hippocampi were like the taxicabs of the sea. They carried sea nymphs and pulled Poseidon's chariot through the water. They were fast swimmers and could travel several miles in the span of just a few seconds.

Kind and helpful by nature, hippocampi were known to rescue those in danger from sea monsters and other maritime threats. Although large and powerful, they were nonviolent creatures, more likely to flee than fight. But in the event of an attack, they used their strong tails and sharp bite to defend themselves.

The name hippocampus comes from the Greek words *hippos*, for "horse," and *kampus*, for "sea monster." With their ability to control the waves and currents of the sea, they were seen as symbols of power and strength, and were portrayed as enormous seahorses.

The human brain has a part called the hippocampus, located in the medial temporal lobe. It is responsible for controlling emotion, regulating the nervous system, and storing memories. This small part of the brain resembles a seahorse, which is why it was given its name.

HIPPOGRIFF

A FAVORITE CREATURE of medieval folklore, hippogriffs were the product of sexual relations between a griffin and a mare. Griffins— part-eagle, part-lion beasts known for their ferocity—were excellent at guarding treasure and other valuables. When griffins weren't hunting humans to feed to their young, they preyed on horses, who were their nemeses that they loved to eat.

For a griffin and a horse to mate was an extremely unusual occurrence, making hippogriffs especially rare and special. They had the body of a horse and the wings, talons, head, and beak of an eagle. They were fast and could be trained, making them useful for knights to use as transportation.

In the last two decades, hippogriffs have reentered popular culture as a result of their inclusion in the Harry Potter book series. In the third book, *Harry Potter and the Prisoner of Azkaban*, students work with hippogriffs in their Care of Magical Creatures class. In this universe, hippogriffs are characterized as being unpleasant to anyone who dares show them disrespect and protective of those who have earned their trust.

HIPPOI ATHANATOI

ALSO KNOWN AS the Hippoi Troiades (horses of Troy), the Hippoi Athanatoi was the name for the group of immortal horses that belonged to the Greek gods. Some sources say the Hippoi Troiades included all the horses of the Greek gods, while others say it contained just the offspring of the wind gods who pulled Zeus's chariot. That would include Boreas, who personified the north wind; Zephryus, the west wind; Notos, the south wind; and Euros, the east wind.

HOFVARPNIR

ONE OF THE fourteen goddesses in Norse legend, Gná was sent by the principal goddess Frigg on errands that took her great distances. She was trusted to deliver messages across the nine worlds. Her trusty steed, Hofvarpnir, was a valuable resource in these tasks, as he could fly through the air and ride on the surface of the sea. The name Hofvarpnir means "hoof kicker."

HORSES OF THE ÆSIR

IN NORSE MYTHOLOGY, the Æsir were a group of gods who comprised the principal pantheon.

They were a benevolent yet powerful tribe who depended on their horses to take them to the Well of Urdr each day for their tribunal. In the *Prose Edda*, a handbook for poets that includes many retellings of classic Norse myths and legends, eleven horses that traveled with the gods are mentioned. They include Gladr, Gyllir, Glenr, Skeidbrimir, Silfrintoppr, Sinir, Gisl, Falhófnir, Gulltoppr, and Léttfeti. The last horse, Sleipnir, is the only one to be associated with a particular deity—Sleipnir belonged to Odin, the god of war.

In Scandinavian culture, horses were believed to have special powers that allowed them to convene with the gods and spirits. In Norse legends, it was not uncommon for a horse to predict the future or to possess innate wisdom that kept its passengers safe.

HORSING AROUND

THE EVERYDAY EXPRESSION "horsing around" is so common that its origins have all but been forgotten. The saying was most likely born from an observation of the way that young horses play—rough and without concern for getting injured. Over time, the expression evolved to include any kind of playful or silly behavior; the association with horselike behavior has faded over time.

HRIMFAXI

THE NORSE GODDESS Nott was known for pulling her chariot through the sky each evening. She was the goddess of night, with dark skin, raven hair, and a black horse to match her shadowy nighttime surroundings. Hrimfaxi was Nott's main horse. As he crossed the evening

sky, he would froth at his bit, sending drops of moisture down to earth to coat the land in what would become the morning dew. According to some sources, Nott's horse also helped to pull the sun across the sky in the daytime.

THE HUMAN-HORSE RELATIONSHIP

HORSES HAVE BEEN domesticated for about six thousand years. In that time, human relationships to horses have shifted and evolved as our way of life has changed. Horses were likely utilized as a food source beginning in prehistoric times, their meat and milk a source of valuable nourishment. But as society developed, so did the interactions between humans and horses. On horseback, people could travel faster and farther than ever before. They could herd their animals much more efficiently than on foot, making it possible to handle four times the amount of livestock. Horses also helped to plow fields, gather harvested crops, and hunt. Valued for their many contributions, humans began to appreciate horses and see them as companions. In turn, horses became more docile and friendly.

Since they were first domesticated, horses have served a variety of purposes in society. The invention of the chariot around 2500 BCE opened up a world of possibilities that were previously unimaginable. Horses could now pull much heavier cargo greater distances. The chariot also changed the way battles were fought, giving an advantage to armies that had the most chariots. Later, chariot racing became a popular sport, with horses pulling chariots in the earliest Olympic games. Betting on games became a beloved tradition that continued even when the sport evolved to our modern-day version of horse racing.

In the twentieth century, horsemanship was becoming more common. Learning the delicate ways of guiding and controlling a horse, as well as mastering its equipment and care, was embraced by horse enthusiasts. Equine-assisted therapy also brought horses and humans together in a new way. Working with horses in a variety of approaches is now commonly used to improve a person's mental and physical well-being.

These days, dog is still man's best friend, but the horse isn't too far behind. Whether horses are competing on a racetrack, being ridden on a trail, or used for therapeutic purposes, the human-horse bond endures.

ICHTHYOCENTAURS

NOT MUCH IS known about the Ichthyocentaurs, or fish centaurs, as most of what we know about them has been gleaned from their presence in ancient Greek art. They were different from Tritons in that they were not simply half-man,

half-fish creatures; rather, they had human tor-
sos, the lower bodies of fish, the forequarters of
a horse, and lobster tails atop their heads like
reindeer antlers.

Siblings to the wise centaur Chiron, only
two Ichthyocentaurs existed in the world.
Their names, Bythos and Aphros (meaning "sea
depths" and "sea-foam," respectively), are a nod
to their undersea ancestry. Aphros was often
depicted as a handsome young man with sea-
foam surrounding his body. Like their brother
Chiron, it is believed that Bythos and Aphros
were capable and trusted mentors.

Some believe that Aphros may have been
a foster father to Aphrodite. In addition to the
similarity in their names, a piece of mosaic art
that remains in Turkey shows the fish-centaur
brothers carrying Aphrodite in her shell.

INKANYAMBA

A LEGENDARY CREATURE in South African folk-lore, Inkanyamba is a sinister serpentine creature with the body of a giant eel and the head of a horse. The beast's details vary, but it is generally agreed upon that Inkanyamba is a huge and dangerous river monster who lives at the bottoms of waterfalls. Some say it is invisible, while others say it has horns and/or wings. Sometimes

described as having seven heads, it has been known to shape-shift into a tornado when looking for a mate.

J

JABUČILO

SURROUNDED BY BREATHTAKING Montenegrin mountain ranges is a lake called Vrazje Jezero, or Devil's Lake. There, as legend has it, a winged horse with a red-tipped coat lives in the water, emerging on starry nights to graze and mate with the nearby female horses. As the tale goes, once the horses have copulated, the winged horse kicks the mare in the side of her stomach in an attempt to prevent pregnancy. One time this plan didn't work, and the result was a foal named

Jabučilo, who later went on to serve Momčilo, a fighter against the Ottomans in the epic folklore of Bulgaria, Serbia, and Herzegovina.

A massive steel and stone statue of Jabučilo was erected in 2017 in Pirot, a city in Serbia. Highlighting the horse's magical qualities, the statue shows Jabučilo with wings extended, as though about to take flight.

K

KANTHAKA

IN INDIAN MYTHOLOGY, Kanthaka is a devoted and faithful equine companion to Prince Siddhartha. Said to have been born on the same day as the prince, the pure-white horse was so loyal that when the prince left his royal

life to go on a spiritual journey (and eventually become
the Buddha), Kanthaka
passed away from heartbreak.

A racehorse named Kanthaka was active
in US **horse racing** (see page 97) from 2018 to

In the United States, an organization called the Jockey Club has the tough task of approving or denying every name that is proposed for a registered horse. There are some rules, like the character limit is eighteen, names must be unique to a horse, and you're not allowed to use vulgar phrases or curse words. People have had a lot of fun over the years coming up with silly names for their horses and it doesn't seem like they'll stop anytime soon. In the eighteenth century, a horse was given the name Potooooooooo. Waikikamukau is another unusual name. Pronounced "Why kick a moo cow," it is a reference to an expression used in New Zealand to describe a faraway, remote place. Sometimes distasteful names do make it past the Jockey Club, like the horse that was allowed to be named Hoof Hearted. (Say it aloud five times fast.)

2021. During his racing career he placed second and third in a handful of races, against such tough competitors as Chewing Gum and Still Having Fun. (Many horses in the sport have notoriously unusual names.) Some of the tracks where he raced include Belmont Park, Keeneland, Kentucky Downs, Santa Anita Park, and Woodbine Racetrack. Born in Kentucky in 2015, Kanthaka was only six years old at retirement. His mother was named Sliced Bread.

KELPIES

A KELPIE IS a shape-shifting sprite that sometimes appears in the form of a horse. Described as having a beautiful black mane and an impressive stature, a kelpie's graceful appearance is a misrepresentation of its true character, which is sometimes described as impish and other times callous or cruel. Kelpies are known to loiter

---
⊚
---

around Scottish rivers and streams, waiting for their next victim. Their method is to trick people (oftentimes children) into hopping on their backs for a friendly trek along a riverbank, only to then jump into the river and drown the unsuspecting riders. In some cases, a kelpie will disembowel its victims, leaving only its entrails behind.

Kelpies are distinguished from horses by having hooves that are inverted. Although mostly described as having a black mane, in one variation kelpies are white. In another, their coats are made of serpents.

KIRAT

KIRAT (ALSO KNOWN as Gyrat or Gi'rot) is the gray horse that belonged to the hero Köroğlu in Turkish and Azerbaijani folklore. In some stories, Köroğlu is a simple robber and trickster. In others, he follows in the tradition of a

Robin Hood—type of character, fighting against inequality for the greater good.

According to legend, Köroğlu's father was blinded by the shah after presenting him with two colts that, although scraggy, had come from magical ancestors. Köroğlu's father assured the shah that they would make fine horses, but the shah was still offended and persisted with doling out punishment. Kirat was one of the two magical colts and went on to become a cherished companion to Köroğlu, who would later avenge his father.

LLAMREI

ACCORDING TO WELSH folklore, King Arthur had a pair of horses named Llamrei and

Hengroen. Llamrei appeared to be the favored
horse, as he was included in more adventures
than Hengroen, and most notable stories place
Llamrei at the center of the action.

King Arthur, from his castle atop a hill,
would survey the land below and make sure
his people were safe. One day he got word that
enemies were approaching, and he jumped into
action. Calling on the Knights of the Round
Table, they set off on horses to defend their
land and people. King Arthur picked the trusty
Llamrei to lead him into battle.

For an entire day, the armies fought bravely.
King Arthur, at once realizing he was out-
numbered and in grave danger, gave his horse
the order to save them both. Llamrei took off,
as fast as lightning, with the enemies at their
backs. He headed straight for the edge of a high
cliff. While the other warriors screeched to a
halt, Llamrei sailed off the cliff. His hooves
slammed into the ground with such force that

a permanent hoofprint was left behind. But the horse and rider were safe, and they galloped away into the distance.

This legend is cited as the explanation for what looks like a hoofprint on a rock in Wales. Called Carn March Arthur, visitors can decide for themselves whether they believe it is indeed a mark left behind by King Arthur's majestic horse.

MAMLAMBO

ACCORDING TO ZULU mythology, Mamlambo, goddess of rivers, is a powerful spirit who lives in South Africa's Mzintlava River. Described as being a gruesome half-fish, half-horse monster, the spirit has a horselike head, a long serpent's body, stumpy legs, and glow-in-the-dark skin, and grows to be almost seventy feet long. In some versions of her story, she is said to be a beautiful woman who lures unsuspecting people into the river, where they are then drowned. In others, Mamlambo is portrayed as wicked and malevolent, sucking the blood and brains out of her victims. And in others still, she is depicted as a tragic figure who was forced to live in the river against her will.

In 1997, at least seven people and many animals went missing along the shores of the Mzintlava River. Mamlambo received the blame for these deaths, which were said to have occurred when a river monster emerged from the water to grab its victims, then pull them back into the river to drown. The deaths remain unexplained. As fearfully regarded as this creature is, many people view Mamlambo as a good-luck charm, with the power to grant wishes, cure the sick, and give wealth to those who are pure of heart. Despite having a polarizing reputation, Mamlambo remains an important and enduring figure in South African society.

THE MARES OF DIOMEDES

THE MARES OF Diomedes were four horses in Greek mythology that fed on human flesh. They belonged to the giant Diomedes, king of Thrace. The names of the mares were Podargos ("swift"), Lampon ("shining"), Xanthos ("yellow"), and Deinos ("terrible").

In the tale of the Labors of Heracles, King Eurystheus tasked Heracles with stealing the Mares of Diomedes. Not knowing that the mares were wild and that they required human flesh for sustenance, Heracles had no idea of the challenges that lay ahead.

There are a few versions of this story. In one, Heracles brings along his friend Abderus

to handle the horses while he fights Diomedes.
After killing the giant, Heracles approaches the
mares, only to realize they have eaten his friend.

In another version, Heracles traps the mares
on a peninsula, which he turns into an island
by digging a trench and filling it with water.
When Diomedes finds them, Heracles kills him

and feeds him to the horses, who become tame after eating.

Heracles does succeed eventually in bringing the mares to Eurystheus, where they either roam the countryside or are killed by wolves and lions, depending on which version of the story you read.

MORVARC'H

IN BRETON MYTHOLOGY, King Gradlon ruled over the city of Ys.

One evening, while he was sleeping, his daughter stole his key to the city's gates. Princess Dahut had planned to sneak her lover into the city, but her plan was not well-thought-out, and when she opened the gates, water from the ocean rushed in. As the city began to flood, the king grabbed his daughter and horse, Morvarc'h, to flee for safer lands. Saint Gwenole, one of the king's spiritual advisers, demanded that he toss his devilish daughter into the water and leave her behind. Reluctantly, the king obeyed and fled the city with just his horse.

But Dahut did not die that day—when she landed in the water after being pushed off Morvarc'h, she transformed into a mermaid. It has been said that she appears to fishers and lures them to their death.

NUCKELAVEE

OFF THE NORTHEASTERN coast of Scotland lies Orkney, an archipelago of about seventy islands with rich history and folklore. The old Orcadians believed in a number of supernatural creatures, but none were as feared as the nuckelavee. This beast, considered by old Orcadians to be evil incarnate, had no skin, a mouth resembling a pig's snout that emanated a putrid odor, a single fiery red eye, and a head ten times the size of a human's. Due to his lack of skin, his flesh appeared raw, with leathery muscles and black blood pumping through his veins. Accounts vary, but some say the beast rode an equally monstrous horse, while others say the two creatures merged into a single grotesque creature.

The nuckelavee lived in the sea but roamed on land freely. He was believed to be so powerful that he could conjure blights, droughts, disasters, and epidemics. He existed solely to torment the Orcadians, who lived in fear of his wrath.

NYKUR

THE NYKUR (OR nennir) is an Icelandic water horse, believed to live in bodies of water, such as lakes, ponds, rivers, and oceans. Evil in nature, they lure unsuspecting victims by appearing to be friendly and tame. Once mounted, however, a rider will find themself stuck like glue to the horse's back, unable to get free. The nykur will then gallop toward the sea, plunging into deep waters and drowning its victim. These cruel creatures are also known to break the surface of frozen lakes to harm people who are ice fishing.

Nykurs are known to change shape, sometimes appearing as a cow or a giant fish. When presenting as a horse, they are usually gray, although pink, white, and gray with spots or streaks have also been reported. They may have red cheeks, short necks, inverted hooves, and one blazing eye.

As terrifying as they can be, there are numerous methods of dealing with nykurs. First, they are safe to ride as long as they are not near water. Second, they hate fire, so keeping a fire going will push a nykur to leave the area. They dislike holy water and can't stand the sound of their own name. To tame a nykur, employ this neat trick: puncture the lump underneath their left shoulder. If this lump is punctured, the nykur becomes harmless, although there is always a possibility that the lump grows back, along with the creature's evil tendencies.

O

THE OLD MAN
WHO LOST HIS HORSE

ONE OF THE most famous ancient Chinese children's fables tells the story of an old man whose only horse ran away. Upon hearing that the old man's horse was gone, his neighbors felt very bad and offered words of comfort.

"We're so sorry," his neighbors said. "That was your only horse. You must be so upset!"

But the old man wasn't upset. "I don't know if it's good or bad," he said. "I just know I don't have my horse."

The next day, the missing horse came back, and he brought with him a **qianlima** (see page 84), a horse that could travel four hundred kilometers (about 250 miles) in a day.

"How exciting!" his neighbors said. "Not only did you get your horse back, but you now have a qianlima, too! You must be so happy!"

But the old man wasn't happy. "I don't know if it's good or bad," he said. "I just know I have two horses."

The next day, the old man's son wanted to ride the qianlima. Being a qianlima, the horse took off like a shot. The horse was too fast and the boy fell off and broke his leg.

"We're so sorry," his neighbors said. "It's terrible that your son broke his leg. You must be so upset!"

But the old man wasn't upset. "I don't know if it's good or bad," he said. "I just know that my son broke his leg."

Soon, a war had started and every able-bodied young man was sent off to fight for his country. The old man's son, however, was injured. He couldn't fight with a broken leg and so he was spared from having to go to war. The war turned out to be terribly brutal and every young man who had gone into battle was killed. But not the old man's son. He escaped death because he had broken his leg. What some considered to be a misfortune turned out to have saved his life.

The lesson the fable teaches is to avoid judging a situation before you really know the outcome. If you give it time, you will see the bigger picture.

P

PEGASUS

ONE OF TWO children born to Medusa and Poseidon, Pegasus was a winged stallion with an independent nature and a wild spirit. Like his father, ruler of the sea, Pegasus had a powerful affinity with the water—he was able to create flowing streams with his hooves. He created Hippocrene, a sacred spring on Mount Helicon that muses drank from for creativity and inspiration. The name Hippocrene translates to "horse fountain."

For a time, Pegasus served as Bellerophon's steed. One of the beloved heroes of the Greek myths, Bellerophon is perhaps best known for slaying the vicious fire-breathing monster Chimera, a feat he could not have executed without Pegasus's

help. Unlike others who had tried and failed to kill Chimera, Bellerophon had the advantage of flight. On Pegasus's back, Bellerophon shot arrows from the air, killing the beast.

Bellerophon triumphed over many enemies with Pegasus's help. His success as a hero eventually led him to believe that consorting with mortals was beneath him. He felt that he belonged on Mount Olympus and set off on Pegasus's back to take his place among the gods. As they ascended the mountain, an angered Zeus sent a gadfly to bite Pegasus. Startled, Pegasus threw Bellerophon from his back, and depending on the source, Bellerophon either descended to his death or fell back down to Earth, badly injured.

Pegasus then sets off on his own to continue the journey that Bellerophon started. When he reaches the heavens, he is welcomed and put to use in Zeus's herd. Proving himself to be loyal, faithful, and hardworking, he is entrusted with the task of pulling the chariot that contains Zeus's thunderbolts and lightning, and Pegasus lives out the rest of his days on Mount Olympus as Zeus's cherished aide.

Pegasus remains relevant today as a symbol of speed, beauty, and artistic vision. He has popped up in many films dating back many decades, including the 1940 film *Fantasia*, the 1997 film *Hercules*, and both the 1981 and 2010 version of *Clash of the Titans*. In the Percy Jackson and the Olympians series, Pegasus is depicted as the father of the other winged horses. Pegasus has also had a huge impact as a marketing and sales tool all over the world. The image of Pegasus conjures grandeur and the idea of the soul escaping the confines of the physical world. It is an appealing image that captivates and motivates people of all ages. That it is successfully and widely used in logos, commercials, and ads is a testament to the universal desire to embody the spirit of Pegasus.

Q

QIANLIMA

LEGENDARY IN EAST Asian countries, the qian-lima (also known as chollima) is a winged horse capable of traveling at very high speeds. Translating to "thousand-li horse," it is said to be able to travel one thousand li (about 310 miles) in just a day without the need for food or water. In China, the word *qianlima* is used to describe an accomplished, talented, or capable person. Much like a horse with startling physical power, a person characterized as having qian-lima is worthy of great respect and admiration.

The qianlima is the national animal of North Korea. In the country's capital, Pyongyang, a large bronze statue of this horse was erected in 1961. It is a symbol of progress, representing a

time when leaders asked the country's workers
to invoke the spirit of the horse to achieve rapid
reconstruction in the wake of the Korean War.

RAKHSH

THE *SHĀH-NĀMEH*, OR *Book of Kings*, tells of the
myths, history, and culture of ancient Persia.
Written by the poet Abolqasem Ferdowsī, it is
the longest piece of literature created by a single
author, containing over fifty thousand rhymed
couplets and 990 chapters.

The horse of the Iranian hero Rustam,
Rakhsh is portrayed as being a strong and capable stallion. As a young man, Rustam showed
potential to be a great warrior and his father

promised to find him a suitable horse. For three years, warriors had tried to catch and tame a wild stallion, without any success. Rustam was the only one who was able to mount the spirited creature. He named Rakhsh after the Persian word for lightning, and together the two would go on many adventures and even head into battle together. With Rakhsh by his side, Rustam was invincible and he emerged as the champion of Iran.

RHAEBUS

MEZENTIUS, THE ETRUSCAN king in Roman myths, was known for his cruel nature and his hatred of the gods. During a battle with Aeneas and the Trojans, Mezentius's son, Lausus, bravely saved his father's life at the expense of his own. When Mezentius discovered that Aeneas had killed his son, he headed back into battle on his horse, Rhaebus, to avenge his son's death. Mezentius managed to avoid Aeneas's spear for a short time but ultimately was struck down, the arrow hitting both his horse and him, ending both of their lives.

Rhaebus is also the name of a genus of metallic bean weevils. At only three to five millimeters in size, these tiny bugs eat only plants in the *Nitraria* genus. They live in the Palearctic region, an area that encompasses Europe, Asia north of the Himalayas, and Africa north of the Sahara.

S

ŠARAC

IN THE LATE fourteenth century, the Serbian prince Marko Kraljević ascended to the throne after his father died in a battle with the Turks. Celebrated for his bravery, chivalry, and integrity, the new king was well-liked, though the details of his life were obscure. It was well-known, however, that he had a close friendship with his horse, named Šarac. Stories of their adventures were recorded in South Slavic songs, epic poems, and folklore.

One legend tells the story of how Kraljević came to own his beloved horse. After many trials with horses that didn't live up to his standards, Kraljević came upon a sick horse that nevertheless appeared to have potential. Like he had done with the others, Kraljević grabbed this horse by its tail and attempted to swing it over his shoulder. When the horse didn't budge, Kraljević knew he had found the one. Once he was cured of his sickness, Kraljević shared his wine with the horse, and from that point on, the two were inseparable.

There are conflicting tales about the death of Kraljević and what came of Šarac. In one popular legend, Kraljević was riding Šarac one morning when the horse stumbled and began crying. Kraljević took this as an omen, and sure enough, a spirit later appeared before him and said it was his time to die. Kraljević accepted this fate and killed and buried his beloved horse so that it could not fall into the hands of his enemies. Afterward, he threw his weapons into the ocean and simply decided to lie down and wait to die.

SIVKO-BURKO

SIVKO-BURKO, A MAGICAL horse that can grant anyone's wish, is featured in a popular Slavic folktale. In the story, a foolish young man named Ivan is preoccupied with his hobby of searching the woods for mushrooms, while his two elder brothers toil on the family's farm. The brothers' father was very sick and, from his deathbed, asked if his sons could bring bread to his grave for three nights in a row after he'd passed.

After their father died, the two elder brothers found excuses to avoid executing their father's last wish. Ivan, however, stayed true to his word. On the first night, the eldest brother asked Ivan to go to their father's grave in his place and Ivan obliged. On the second night, the middle brother asked Ivan to go to their father's grave in his place and Ivan again obliged. On the third night, he asked his brothers if one

of them might go in his place, as he was tired
from the last two nights. But again, Ivan ends
up visiting his father on his own, bringing the
bread that was requested. Each night, his father,
appearing as a ghost, eats the bread and talks
to his son. On the last night, he gives his son
instructions to summon the horse Sivko-Burko,
who has the power to make Ivan handsome.

That same night, the tsar issued a procla-
mation, summoning all the single men to his
courtyard to compete for his daughter's hand
in marriage. Ivan's brothers dress in their finest
and leave their youngest brother behind. Ivan,
taking his chances, summons Sivko-Burko to
make him handsome for the tsar's party. In an
open field, the horse appears and transforms
Ivan into the most handsome man. On Sivko-
Burko's back, Ivan rides to the tsar's courtyard, where his brothers and all the other single
men in the kingdom are gathered. Appearing
as this handsome young man, Ivan catches the

attention of the princess, who leaves a shining mark on his forehead.

The next day, everyone in the kingdom is summoned to the castle for a banquet. The princess and the tsar walk person to person, trying to find the dashing man from the previous night. Finally, they reached Ivan, who is disheveled and dirty, looking nothing like he did the night before, with a rag tied around his head to hide the blinding mark. The princess asks him to remove the rag, and when he does the whole room lights up from her mark on Ivan's forehead. But the princess and her father want to know why he looks so different. Ivan then goes outside to call upon Sivko-Burko once again. When Ivan reenters the castle, the princess recognizes him immediately as the handsome man from the previous night. Joyously, the tsar announces that they have found a husband for the princess and all are invited to the wedding.

SIVUSHKO

IN RUSSIAN LEGEND, a magical horse named
Sivushko was said to run like the wind and
jump over mountains in a single leap. Its
owner, the knight Il'ya Muromets, was lucky
to have such a remarkable horse. In one story,
Il'ya and Sivushko traveled two hundred miles
in just three hours to reach a camp where forty
thousand robbers had gathered. As the horse
skillfully navigated through the crowd, Il'ya
was able to strike down every single robber
with his sword.

SKINFAXI

IN NORSE MYTHOLOGY, giants were a race of
beings who had supernatural powers and flaws,
just like Norse gods. Two giants named Dag
and Nott pulled the sun and moon each day,

bringing lightness and darkness to Earth. Dag had a horse named Skinfaxi, who was known to be the best of the horses. Skinfaxi was powerful and majestic, with the ability to run faster than any other horse. Some stories describe his coat as golden. His name means "shining mane," and his gleam brought light to the heavens and Earth. He was often associated with the beauty of nature and the power of the sun. (Read about Nott's horse, **Hrimfaxi**, on page 53.)

SLEIPNIR

SLEIPNIR, THE MOST well-known horse in Norse mythology, belonged to the great war god, Odin. He had an advantage over other horses, in that he had eight legs that could carry him faster than any other horse. In some stories, he is described as being incredibly large, and in others, he's just a bit larger than a regular horse.

But by all accounts, he was an incredibly loyal and valuable companion to Odin.

According to the *Prose Edda*, an ancient Norse text, Sleipnir's birth was the result of one of Loki's tricks. The trickster god turned himself into a beautiful mare to distract a stallion named Svadilfari from his work, but he did not expect Svadilfari to pursue him in the form of

a mare so ardently. Svadilfari impregnated the mare, and Sleipnir was the unintended offspring of this union.

In one of the most well-known stories in Norse folklore, Odin has unsettling dreams and travels with Sleipnir to Hel, the world of the dead, to get answers. Hel is surrounded by a high wall to keep the dead inside and the living outside. Sleipnir, with his ability to travel between dimensions, easily hops the wall with Odin on his back. Once inside, Odin receives the terrible news that his son would soon be entering the realm of the dead. Devastated, Odin and Sleipnir ride back to Asgard to stop the foretold events from unfolding. Later, Sleipnir would find himself traveling to Hel once again, this time carrying Hermod, a messenger of the gods. After a long journey, they face the same problem that Odin faced— Hermod as a living person, is not able to enter Hel. On Sleipnir's back, however, they make it over the wall, and Hermod is able to complete his mission.

THE SPORT OF HORSE RACING

THE ORIGINS OF horse racing trace back to the Roman Empire, when chariot and mounted races were held for public entertainment. The concept was simple: Two horses raced a set distance to determine which was faster. Despite the straightforwardness of the sport, it has remained virtually unchanged to this day and continues to entertain audiences around the world.

In the United States, the biggest horse racing event is the Kentucky Derby, which attracts more than 150,000 fans to the Churchill Downs racetrack in Louisville, Kentucky, in May of each year. The race, which has been held since 1875, is well-known for certain traditions.

Almost every spectator wears a hat, and the women's hats are known to be especially extravagant. Participants sip mint juleps, a cocktail made with bourbon. And they snack on hot browns, an open-faced turkey sandwich with bacon and cheese.

In order to make it to the Kentucky Derby, horses must earn top marks in a series of races. Only twenty horses with the highest scores will make it to the Kentucky Derby, where the top winner stands to take home a handsome monetary prize. In 2022, the first-place winnings reached $1.86 million.

About three hundred years ago, thoroughbred racing became a popular sport in England, where it was common for royalty to take an interest in breeding the most exceptional horses. This is how thoroughbred racing became known as the "sport of kings."

Belmont Stakes and Preakness Stakes are two other significant annual events in the world of horse racing. Along with the Kentucky Derby, the three events together are known as the American Classics. A special prize called the Triple Crown is awarded to a horse that comes in first place in all three races. Only eleven horses have managed to accomplish this feat in the sport's history.

Horse betting is a common practice at horse racing events. These days, you don't even have to attend an event to be able to bet on it—different apps and websites allow users to place their bets online.

STRAIGHT FROM THE HORSE'S MOUTH

WHEN SOMEONE SAYS they heard something "straight from the horse's mouth," you can be sure the information is coming from the very best source, and that the intel is reliable and sound. The expression comes from the practice of examining a horse's mouth to determine its age and health. Younger horses have fewer teeth and a less developed jaw. A glance at the teeth will give an equine expert a good sense of a horse's age. This information is used to determine a horse's worth when being sold, or as an indicator of how well a horse will do in a race, which is critical in deciding whether to bet on it.

SVADILFARI

WHEN THE NORSE gods decided to build a wall around Asgard, a builder offered his services in exchange for the sun, the moon, and the goddess Freya. The gods were not keen on his offer, until Loki, the trickster god, convinced them it was a good idea. The gods had two stipulations. First, if the work was not done in three seasons, the builder would not be paid. Second, the builder must complete the job without help from another man. The builder inquired about using his horse, Svadilfari, to aid in the building of the wall, and with some additional cajoling by Loki, the gods at last agreed.

What they didn't know was that Svadilfari was a huge asset to the builder. The horse was able to move heavy stones great distances quickly. As they approached the deadline for the wall, it was looking like the builder and his hardworking horse would indeed be finished in time. This presented a problem for the gods, who did not want to give up Freya, the sun, and the moon. Angry with Loki for getting them into this predicament, the gods told Loki it would be his responsibility to deal with, or he would face death.

Loki concocted a plan to distract Svadilfari so that the horse could not complete the wall. Transforming himself into a beautiful mare, Loki put himself in the path of Svadilfari, who was instantly mesmerized by Loki's beauty. The mare took off into the woods and Svadilfari followed. All night long Svadilfari looked for the mare, and by the next day, the deadline for completing the wall had passed. Nevertheless, he would not give up his search. He eventually caught up to Loki (still appearing as the attractive mare) and overpowered her. The magical eight-legged horse, **Sleipnir** (see page 94), was later born to Loki.

T

THREE-FOOT HORSE

THE THREE-FOOT HORSE of Caribbean folklore
appears as a horse with two back legs and only
one front leg. Despite missing an appendage,
the horse is a very fast runner. Ridden by a figure known as the whooping boy, the three-foot
horse is a type of duppy, meaning a spirit or evil
entity, a concept that originated in West Africa
and was carried to the Caribbean with the slave
trade. With its red eyes and hot flaming breath,
the three-foot horse is a fearsome beast. Believed
to be the spirit of a young enslaved boy who had
endured great suffering, the whooping boy was
no less terrifying than his steed, and together
they struck fear in the hearts of everyone they
encountered. The whooping boy carried a whip

and also could kill with his blazing breath. The horse and the whooping boy were known to come out at night—the *"yip, yip"* call of the boy was a warning that danger was near. One way to stay safe from the three-foot horse is to stay out of the moonlight; they don't attack in the pitch-black dark.

TIANMA

OFTEN CONFUSED WITH Pegasus, Tianma is a winged horse from Chinese folklore that lives on Horse-Succeeds Mountain. Tianma translates to "sky horse"—the word *sky* in Chinese meaning both the literal sky as well as the idea of the heavens. Often described as looking like a white dog with a black head, it fears humans and will fly away if it encounters one.

The annual Tianma International Tourism Festival takes place in northwest China's

Xinjiang Uygur autonomous region. The celebration of horse culture attracts people from all over the world.

Events include horse races, workshops, and discussion panels, but the highlight of the event is the stunning scene when they set free thousands of horses at once to gallop exuberantly across a bright green meadow.

TIKBALANG

A TIKBALANG IS a demon from Philippine folklore that was said to have long, stretched human limbs and the head of a horse. Usually described as being covered in black fur, a white tikbalang is rare but thought to be especially magical. Tikbalangs can take on any shape and form, including that of a human. They reportedly live in the mountains, where they lead travelers astray for fun.

Stories of tikbalangs are often told to children as a warning to not venture too far from home at night. It is said that they wait in tall trees for a traveler to come by and then impersonate someone the traveler knows. One way to know if someone is actually a tikbalang in disguise is to notice if he or she smells like smoke. Tikbalangs are known to be big smokers, and the smell will linger even if they change form. One of the more brutal things they are known to do is capture women, keep them in bamboo cages, and eventually murder them. It was said that when it rains while the sun is shining, that means a tikbalang is getting married.

THE TROJAN HORSE

IN THE PRESENT day, a Trojan horse brings to mind computer malware that appears safe but can cause damage and wreak havoc on a computer. The term *Trojan horse* is used to describe scenarios in which someone is planning a secret attack on an enemy by infiltrating a group or institution to bring it down from the inside. Both of these concepts were born from the story of the Trojan horse in Homer's *Iliad* and *Odyssey*.

The cause of the Trojan War has been debated, but the most traditionally accepted version is that Paris (the son of King Priam, the Trojan ruler) and Helen (the wife of the Greek ruler, King Menelaus) fell in love and ran away together to Troy. Menelaus,

upset about losing Helen, the most beautiful
woman in the world, persuades his brother,
Agamemnon, to put together an army of Greek
warriors to battle Troy.

The war that ensued lasted for ten years.
At the end, the Greeks hatched a shrewd plan.
They built a large wooden structure in the
shape of a horse and offered it to Athena as a
gift. Ignoring her advisers, Athena accepted the
gift, and the horse was let into Troy.

Later that night, Greek warriors emerged
from inside the hollow wooden structure and

unlocked Troy's gates, where the rest of the Greek army was waiting. Almost all of Troy's inhabitants were murdered that night, and the town was destroyed. Troy fell, and Helen was taken back to Greece.

TULPAR

TULPAR IS THE legendary winged horse of Turkic mythology, believed to be an amalgamation of two animals essential to the nomadic life of the people of Central Asia, the horse and the eagle. At that time, hunting was a crucial part of life. Hunters would bring along horses and eagles or other birds of prey on hunts. The eagle was thought to keep away evil spirits, as well as to invoke strength and righteousness. Horses played an essential role in their society as well; in addition to being useful in hunting, these nomadic people depended on horses to move from place to place. Over time, the image of the horse and the eagle merged into a single significant entity, which became the Tulpar. To this day, it is an important symbol in Central Asia. Tulpar's image is used on both the Mongolian state emblem and the state emblem of the Republic of Kazakhstan.

UCHCHAIHSHRAVAS

IN HINDU MYTHOLOGY, there is a seven-headed horse known as Uchchaihshravas. As white as snow and able to fly, he was known as the king of horses and belonged to Indra, the king of the gods. Although this is the more popular belief, it has also been said that Uchchaihshravas belonged to King Bali, otherwise known as the king of the demons.

Uchchaihshravas means "loud neighing." Legend has it that he was created during the churning of the milky ocean, in a time before humankind existed, when the ocean was made from the milk of Mother Earth.

UNICORN

THE BENEVOLENT UNICORN, with its pure, peaceful demeanor and magical spiral horn, has captured the hearts and imaginations of many. Believed to have originated in Greek myths, a unicorn is usually depicted with a horse's body and a single horn growing from its forehead. The unicorn represents purity and beauty and is cherished in many cultures. Unlike most other mythological creatures that conjure grotesque, beastly images, the unicorn is universally thought to be benevolent and good-hearted.

Among its many magical traits, unicorns are said to walk so softly that their hooves don't make a sound. Their horns are thought to have superb healing qualities—by ingesting their horn or wearing their leather, viruses and other illnesses can be healed. They are also said to be able to purify water, eliminating any poison it may contain and making it safe to drink.

Medieval people believed the unicorn was real, in part because narwhal horns were discovered and thought to be parts of long-gone unicorns. These horns were prized possessions, as people believed them to have the magical ability to protect against or cure poisonings.

The unicorn has been a popular subject in art and literature for centuries. In recent years, unicorns have been a fixture in pop culture and have been the subject of many movies, TV shows, and books. They feature prominently

In Chinese mythology, the qilin is a unicorn that appears at the birth or death of someone who was or will be a great sage. Indian mythology, too, has a version of a unicorn, called ekashringa.

in the television series *My Little Pony: Friendship Is Magic*, as well as the popular cartoon *Adventure Time*. Many books, like the popular *Phoebe and Her Unicorn* graphic novel series, have unicorn main characters. And unicorn fever has even extended to food and drink. The limited edition Unicorn Frappuccino at Starbucks, as well as countless unicorn cakes and cookies, have blown up on social media sites like Instagram and Facebook.

W

WHITE HORSE OF KENT

A HISTORICAL SYMBOL associated with Kent, a county of England, the White Horse of Kent is also called Invicta, which means unconquerable in Latin. The origins of the symbol are debated, but one popular theory is that Hengist, the Anglo-Saxon leader who founded Kent, carried a battle flag with an image of the Saxon Steed. We do know that the nickname Invicta came about in 1066 when the people of Kent thwarted attempts by William the Conqueror to occupy their land. The symbol has only gained significance since then.

The flag of Kent bears an image of a white horse rearing up on a red background. According to the Flag Institute, the UK's national flag

charity, the use of the White Horse of Kent on the county's flag dates back to the seventeenth century. More recently, it has been used to represent institutions in Kent, such as the police, the university, and the county council. The emblem also appears on the coat of arms of a region in northwest Germany called Lower Saxony.

WIDOW-MAKER

TALES OF THE folk hero Pecos Bill have been told
since people began to settle in America's West.
According to legend, Bill was born in the 1830s,
the youngest of eighteen children. When he was
very young, he was separated from his family
when he fell into the water as they were crossing
the Pecos River. He was adopted and raised by
coyotes, who taught him courage, independence,
and strength. Tales of Bill's phenomenal feats
spread and evolved as the stories were shared.
He was known to be quite brave and wild,
too—he liked to ride the turbulent winds of a
cyclone and used a rattlesnake as a whip.

Stories about Pecos Bill oftentimes revolved
around his incredible strength and prowess as
a rodeo rider and horse wrangler. Pecos Bill's
favorite horse was called Widow-Maker. The
name comes from the idea that the horse was so
dangerous to ride that it could make a widow

out of the rider's spouse. Having tamed many wild animals in his day, Bill was the perfect owner for a horse that liked to eat dynamite.

During his courtship with a woman named Slue-Foot Sue, Bill reluctantly agreed to let her ride Widow-Maker. Upset at being shared, the horse bucked Slue-Foot Sue off, sending her bouncing off his back. It has been said that she bounced all the way to the moon—and might still be bouncing to this day.

Unfortunately, even tough, strong cowboys like Pecos Bill don't live forever. According to legend, he died from eating barbed wire and drinking nitroglycerin.

WINDHORSE

IN TIBETAN TRADITION, brightly colored prayer flags are printed with symbols and prayers and hung outside so that the wind can deliver good fortune to people everywhere. Dating back to ancient Buddhist India, the flags come in sets of five and are hung in a particular order: starting on the left, the blue flag is first, followed by white, red, green, and yellow. Each color represents a different element—blue for the sky and space, white for the air and wind, red for fire, green for water, and yellow for earth. Prayer flags printed with an image of a windhorse are the most common type. In the center

of the flag, there is a horse, which represents speed and the ability to transform bad luck to good luck. On the horse's back, three flaming jewels represent the Buddha, Dharma (Buddhist teachings), and sangha (the Buddhist community). All around the horse, Tibetan prayers and mantras are written, and around the perimeter of the flag, powerful Buddhist symbols represent the path to enlightenment. When hanging Tibetan prayer flags, it's important to do so with the pure intention of bringing happiness to everyone everywhere.

Z

ZODIAC HORSE

IN THE CHINESE zodiac, the twelve signs are represented by animals. Every year corresponds to an animal, and they cycle in this order: Rat, Ox, Tiger, Rabbit, Dragon, Snake, Horse, Goat, Monkey, Rooster, Dog, and Pig. The animal sign for a person's birth year is believed to influence their personality and destiny.

People born in the Year of the Horse are said to be agile and strong and have a good work ethic. They are also known for their intelligence, compassion, and independence. Excellent at communicating and performing, Horse signs have a magnetism that draws people to them. They can also, however, be seen as self-centered and impulsive at times, when their determination and action-oriented tendencies go unchecked.

ZULJANAH

THE BATTLE OF Karbala was an important conflict in the history of Islam. The story that explains the events leading up to the battle, the details of the battle, and the aftermath has been passed down for generations. The skirmish occurred on October 10, in the year 680, in the area that is now modern-day Iraq. Imam al-Ḥusayn ibn ʿAlī, the grandson of the Prophet Muhammad, led a small army against the first Muslim dynasty, the Umayyads. Husayn's faithful steed, Zuljanah, tried to protect his master and other followers from harm. Unsuccessful in his efforts, a defeated Zuljanah was left to wander alone, becoming a symbol of devotion for the Shia Muslims, who mourn those lost on the anniversary of the battle every year.

In 2021, Iran began testing of a satellite launcher called Zuljanah, named for the horse that belonged to Imam al-Ḥusayn ibn ʿAlī. The long-range ballistic launcher is said to weigh fifty-two tons and stand almost eighty-six feet high. It has become a concern for other nations who fear its use in launching nuclear warheads.

CONCLUSION

E ven in the earliest of civilizations, horses have been featured prominently in the myths, legends, and folklore of most, if not all, cultures. The wide range of how horses are depicted in these stories is staggering—in some tales they're murderous and in others they grant wishes. Sometimes they're magnificent, with beautiful, shiny manes and other times so ugly that their skinless frames reveal the muscles and blood pumping inside. Some can fly or travel miles in a single jump while others are missing a limb. Possibly the only thing these characters have in common is that they are revered and respected.

We can learn a lot about early civilizations by studying their folklore, and one thing is clear: Horses have always been objects of admiration and curiosity. Considering the influence of horses on ancient cultures, especially in the areas of agriculture, warfare, and transportation, it makes sense that an appreciation of horses is woven into their stories.

Even non-mythical horses today enjoy having many equine fans. Every generation seems to discover horses anew, loving them for the reasons people have adored them throughout the ages: for their physical prowess and speed, their untamed spirit, and their immense beauty and grace.

WORKS CITED

Bane, Theresa. *Encyclopedia of Beasts and Monsters in Myth, Legend and Folklore.* Jefferson, NC: McFarland & Company, 2016.

Bartlett, Sarah. *The Mythology Bible: The Definitive Guide to Legendary Tales.* New York: Union Square & Co., 2009.

Busby, Debbie, and Catrin Rutland. *The Horse: A Natural History.* Princeton, NJ: Princeton University Press, 2019.

Cotterell, Arthur, and Rachel Storm. *The Illustrated Encyclopedia of World Mythology.* London: Anness Publishing, 2017.

Daniels, Mark. *World Mythology in Bite-Sized Chunks.* London: Michael O'Mara Books, 2016.

DeAngelo, Debra. *The Elements of Horse Spirit: The Magical Bond Between Humans and Horses.* Woodbury, MN: Llewellyn Worldwide, 2020.

Doniger, Wendy. *Winged Stallions and Wicked Mares: Horses in Indian Myth and History.* Charlottesville, VA: University of Virginia Press, 2021.

WORKS CITED

The Editors of DK. *The Mythology Book: Big Ideas Simply Explained.* New York: DK Publishing, 2018.

Giesecke, Annette. *Classical Mythology A to Z: An Encyclopedia of Gods & Goddesses, Heroes & Heroines, Nymphs, Spirits, Monsters, and Places.* Philadelphia: Running Press, 2020.

Hausman, Gerald, and Loretta Hausman. *The Mythology of Horses: Horse Legend and Lore Throughout the Ages.* New York: Three Rivers Press, 2003.

Howey, Oldfield M. *The Horse in Magic and Myth.* Mineola, NY: Dover Publications, 2002.

Rosen, Brenda. *The Mythical Creatures Bible: The Definitive Guide to Legendary Beings.* New York: Union Square & Co., 2009.

Walker-Meikle, Kathleen. *The Horse Book: Horses of Historical Distinction.* New York: Bloomsbury Publishing, 2017.

INDEX

INDEX

ABOUT THE AUTHOR

ELIZA BERKOWITZ is a writer and editor. Her favorite mythical horse is Gringolet, who had a reputation for wearing fanciful clothing and sparkling gold adornments. Her least favorite mythical horse is the tikbalang, with its terrifying appearance and wily nature. She lives in Redding, Connecticut, with her husband and daughter.

ABOUT THE ILLUSTRATOR

KATE FORRESTER is a freelance illustrator from the south coast of England. She specializes in creating bespoke hand-lettering and intricate illustrations for book covers, packaging, and many other applications. More than anything, Kate loves telling stories and collaborating with her clients and authors to bring their words to life.